# JOURNEY TO JESUS

## REV. JERRY C. CROSSLEY

Copyright ©2022 by Rev. Jerry C. Crossley (Higher Ground Books & Media)
All rights reserved. No part of this publication may be reproduced in any form, stored in a retrieval system, or transmitted in any form, or by any means (electronic, mechanical, photocopying, recording or otherwise) without prior permission by the copyright owner and the publisher of this book.

Scripture taken from the HOLY BIBLE, NEW INTERNATIONAL VERSION®. NIV®. Copyright © 1973, 1975, 1984 by International Bible Society. Used by permission of Zondervan. All rights reserved worldwide.

Higher Ground Books & Media
P.O. Box 2914
Springfield, OH 45501-2914
www.highergroundbooksandmedia.com
1-937-970-0554

Because of the dynamic nature of the Internet, any web addresses or links contained in this book may have changed since publication and may no longer be valid. The views expressed in the work are solely those of the author and do not necessarily reflect the views of the publisher, and the publisher hereby disclaims any responsibility for them.

Any people depicted in stock imagery are being used for illustrative purposes only.

ISBN (Paperback): 978-1-955368-18-6

Printed in the United States of America 2022

# JOURNEY TO JESUS

## REV. JERRY C. CROSSLEY

## Dedication

This essay is dedicated to Danielle Lynn Adams. She is our first grandchild, our one and only granddaughter, the mother of our first great grandson, the mother of our first great granddaughter, my own personal soulmate, and besides all of this, a fellow pilgrim, devoutly making her own "Journey to Jesus."

For once He said, "Come unto me, all ye that labor and are heavy laden, and I will give you rest. Take my yoke upon you, and learn of me; for I am meek and lowly in heart: and ye shall find rest unto your souls. For my yoke is easy, and my burden is light." (Matthew 11:28-30 KJV)

~ Rev. Jerry C. Crossley ("Pop")

## Prologue

One evening I was lounging in our cozy living room with a beloved friend and pastor, Dr. Roy Lewis, whose insights, discernment, and profound wisdom I have always treasured. He said, "Now Jerry, you have read many books about Jesus. You know what various scholars have concluded regarding New Testament history, theology, Christology and eschatology. You know, and can repeat, what *they* say. But what do *you* say?"

That was an intensely serious question, echoing Jesus' own challenge to His disciples, "Who do *you* say I am?" (Matthew 16:15). Their personal answer was crucial to their relationship. Roy continued, "You seem to know what everyone *else* thinks about Jesus, but what do *you* think about him? I mean, look, you are holding all of these fragmented pieces of the puzzle, but have you ever tried putting them together to make a complete picture? It's a task I think you should undertake. The result need not be strictly historical or chronological, or an exercise in Biblical scholarship, but it needs to be real in your own life. So, I encourage you to try it. Maybe you can call it something like *Journey to Jesus*."

To my best recollection, that's what Dr. Roy Lewis said. I could not joke my way out of his challenge or make light of it. He reminded me that I did *not* have to include everything, just what impressed itself on my heart and mind. I thought hard about it, and concluded that it would be a helpful exercise for myself to make a composite picture of Christ. I'd entitle it... "Journey to Jesus."

At the conclusion of one of the books in the Hebrew Bible (what Christians call the "Old Testament") we read these words: "Of making many books there is no end, and much study wearies the body." (Ecclesiastes 12:12b NIV)

And at the conclusion of John's Gospel (in the "New Testament") come these words: "Jesus did many other things as well. If every one of them were written down I suppose that even the whole world would not have room for the books that would be written." (John 21:25 NIV)

So, instead of another book, why not just a little booklet, simply, "Journey to Jesus"?

# Journey To Jesus

First, I am a believer in "The Big Bang" theory. I acknowledge that there is a God who created everything, who generated space and time, who spun the galaxies into the expanding universe. He is, therefore, the God who is beyond the limitations of time and space, a multi-dimensional Creator who also made you and me. Here, on this tiny planet, this "little blue dot," we came to life. How and why did all of this come about? Science and religion are asking two different questions apart from one another. Science asks, "*What* happened?" but religion asks, "*Why* did it happen?" Both approaches are valid.

When this Creator chose to make himself known to His creatures, He revealed himself in one human being. I would imagine that if God wanted to reveal Himself to clams, He would have to become a fellow clam! However, He chose to reveal himself to us humans, and took on human form.

Who was that human? Jesus. He is the ultimate destination for our journey. We are trying to reach Him. We use the big word "incarnation" to express the act of God's enfleshing himself in a human body. It seems an odd choice. God appeared to us in a very common and ordinary Jewish construction worker. St. Paul the Apostle would later be moved to write that when the fullness of time arrived (in other words, at just the right moment), God sent His Son (Galatians 4:4). When we look at this Jesus through the eyes of the Gospel writers, we see what God is like.

How? I thought of this analogy (and remember, all analogies are imperfect). Suppose you visited a Native American tribe, somewhere in the Midwest, and sometime in the early 19th century. You sat with them and tried to describe the ocean. Now, this was in the days before photography, so you could not show them a picture of the sea.

You tried to describe how majestic this ocean is, but they stared blankly.

Then, one day, you made the journey back to the East Coast. You walked to the water's edge and filled a jar with the incoming wave. Then you tightly secured the lid, and returned to the reservation. You showed the tribesmen this jar, and to the best of your ability, explained where and how you retrieved it. Then you announced, with deep satisfaction, "Friends, this is the ocean."

Was your statement accurate? Well, yes and no. Certainly, the jar was filled with ocean water, and in observing it, your audience would learn and understand some of its properties. They could shake the jar and notice how the water foams. They could taste the water and note its saltiness, but they were not seeing the Atlantic Ocean in all of its expanse and surging power, with cresting waves and pounding surf. They learned something about the ocean, but certainly not everything. Everything in the jar is ocean, but obviously the whole ocean is not in the jar.

So it is with the incarnation. When people look at Jesus, they could learn some things *about* God, but not everything. For instance, they could see God's love and grace, but not all of His power. Jesus was a finite human being. He could not reveal God's omnipotence, His omniscience, His omnipresence, etc. Jesus could be at only one place at a time, but He could show them God's steadfast love and concern. Jesus was filled with God, but not all of God was in Jesus, just like not all of the ocean was in your jar.

Jesus revealed God's personality. Dr. Armstrong, head of the history department at my college, was lecturing on the origin and development of the Church. He said to us, "I personally think that the Christian faith began on that day when a disciple took a second look at Jesus and said to himself, 'God must be like that!'" St. Paul simply said (2 Corinthians 4:6 NIV) "For God, who said, 'Let light shine out of darkness,' made His light shine in our hearts to give us the light of the knowledge of the glory of God in the face of Christ."

Reflecting on our Christian faith that we share in common, we are aware that it centers upon three wonderful, magical mysteries. First, there is the mystery of the Incarnation: How did God the Creator somehow become man the creature? How did he embody himself in human form? That is the essential mystery of Christmas.

Secondly, there is the mystery of the Atonement: How did one man's shameful death on a cross manage to bring forgiveness, even two thousand years later, to us? That is the lingering mystery of Good Friday.

Thirdly, there is the mystery of the Resurrection: How did one man's triumph over death offer us the assurance of eternal life? That is the abiding mystery of Easter.

I rediscovered a seldom-sung hymn in an old Methodist hymnal (at least I never sang it). Each of its three verses describes one of these mysteries. The words were written by Harry Webb Farrington:

"I know not how that Bethlehem's babe
Could in the God-head be;
I only know the manger child
Has brought God's life to me.

"I know not how that Calvary's cross
A world from sin could free;
I only know its matchless love
Has brought God's love to me.

"I know not how that Joseph's tomb

Could solve death's mystery;
I only know a living Christ,
Our immortality."[1]

Usually, we can't bring ourselves to accept "mystery." We want proof. In fact, we demand it. In my neighborhood in Philadelphia, there was a Lutheran pastor, Martin Wiznat, who touched many lives with the power of God's Word. I did not attend his church, but as a skeptical college student, I asked if I could meet with him, and he agreed. So one night, under cover of darkness, I – like Nicodemus (John 3:1-2) – came to talk with this charismatic preacher.

As I sat with him, I boldly decided to "cut to the chase" and announced, "I want you to prove God to me." He chuckled and said, "Son, I can't prove God to you. No one can 'prove' God to anybody, but if you open your heart and mind to him, God will prove himself to you. The Christian faith has a self-authenticating validity." He went on to remind me that we each need faith in order to live our life. When, for instance, we prepare to cross a heavily trafficked street, we have no guarantee that we'll make it across, but we venture forth as an act of faith. Finally, he added, "A Greek philosopher, Archimedes, once said, 'Give me a point, and I will move the universe.' You see, he needed a starting point, and that starting point is God."

So, Saint Paul wrote in his first letter to the Christians in Corinth, "Where is the wise man? Where is the scholar? Where is the philosopher of this age? Has not God made foolish the wisdom of the world? For since in the wisdom of God the world through its wisdom did not know Him, God was pleased through the foolishness of what was preached to save those who believe. Jews demand miraculous signs and Greeks look for wisdom, but we preach Christ crucified: a stumbling block to Jews and foolishness to Gentiles, but to those whom God has called, both Jews and Greeks, Christ the power of God and the wisdom of God. For the foolishness of God is wiser than man's wisdom, and the weakness of God is stronger than man's strength." (1 Corinthians 1:20-25 NIV). We need a starting point, whether we be Jew or Gentile, and Jesus is that starting point.

   I was a student in Harvard Divinity School, Cambridge, Massachusetts. One evening, a professor with whom I felt close, Dean Samuel Miller, stopped beside me in the hallway and asked, "How are things going, Jerry?" "Fine, fine. I'm getting all As and Bs in my classes." Things, however, weren't really going "fine" in my life. My thoughts were all scrambled, and I was a mess. "No," he said. "I asked you a very serious question, and you were evasive. How are things *really* going for you?" "Terrible," I admitted. "The more I learn, the less I know. I just can't connect the dots. I can't grasp this Christian faith, and I can't understand this God."

   He listened very carefully before he replied. Then he said, "Well, maybe you and I are temperamentally different from each other, but as for me, rather than having a faith so small that I can grasp hold of it, I'd rather have a faith so large and magnetic that it could grasp hold of me. And rather than having a God so small that I, with my finite brain, could understand Him, I'd much prefer to have a God so infinite that he could understand me." Having said this, Dean Miller just turned and walked away, but he had changed my whole perspective. Here I was, trying so hard to get a handle on God, when all I had to do was invite Him to get a handle on me.

I walked back to my dormitory room where, in the darkness, I prayed. I said, "Dear God, I honestly don't know if you are real or not. For all I know, this is just a dramatic monologue and I'm talking to the wall, but if you're real, please help me. Please come into my life and manage it, for I can't manage it myself. Please take hold of my life and do something with it. Please forgive my sin, my overarching and incorrigible selfishness, my constant, continual and irrepressible self-centeredness. Please forgive me."

And then in the warm and caressing silence, without understanding exactly why I was saying the very next words I spoke, I added, "and thank you for dying on the cross for me. Thank you for including me. Please come into my life and help me to become the person you created me to be." Without realizing it, I had paraphrased what Evangelicals call "The Sinner's Prayer." My conflict was over. At last, I knew, in the depths of my soul, that the Lord is real. The secret of this faith lies not in our grasping Him, but in His grasping us.

We do that through prayer. Admittedly, when I pray, I present God with an agenda. I not only tell Him what the problem is, I suggest to Him how to fix it. Usually, nothing much happens as a result of my negotiations. Instead, it is probably more effective to spend time *listening* to the Lord, waiting upon His agenda for us, instead of pushing *our* agenda for Him. When I make my mind blank and intentionally listen, in the listening silence I am not expecting to hear back a thunderous voice or a little pip-squeak voice. Instead, I will experience a counter-intuitive prompting, a "God nudge," that will direct me. Wordlessly, He leads me.

One poet wrote:

"Speak to Him, thou, for He hears,
And Spirit with Spirit can meet –
Closer is He than breathing,
And nearer than hands and feet."

("The Higher Pantheism," stanza 6; Alfred, Lord Tennyson)

He brushes past us and calls our name. He chooses us to be His hands and feet. He met His first disciples on the lakeside, working as commercial fishermen, and promised that they would fulfill His expectations by becoming fishers of people. (They catch them, and the Holy Spirit cleans them!) We are to imitate Jesus, offering others a brand-new way of loving, of living, of reconciling, of forgiving, of building bridges instead of walls.

Eugene H. Peterson, in "The Message" (the Bible in contemporary language), wrote this paraphrase of 2 Corinthians 5:16-20: "Now we look inside, and what we see is that anyone united with the Messiah gets a fresh start, is created new. The old life is gone; a new life burgeons! Look at it! All this comes from the God who settled the relationship between us and Him, and then called us to settle our relationships with each other. God has given us the task of telling everyone what He is doing. We're Christ's representatives. God uses us to persuade men and women to drop their differences and enter into God's work of making things right between them. We're speaking for Christ himself now. Become friends with God. He's already become a friend with you."

Reconciliation: making up. You know what stands in our way of doing this? I'll just take a wild guess: our pride. I never saw pride help anyone. Self-esteem, yes; pride, no. Someone once said that in the middle of the word "pride" is that one little letter that always gives us so much trouble. It has certainly been true in my life. I had a friend named Stosh (Stanley Dlugosz), an all-American, simultaneously, in two sports during college. He was a genuinely good and kind person, with a magnetic personality. Gradually, my group of friends coalesced around him (instead of me!), and I became jealous. I found an opportunity to question his motives and to challenge his integrity regarding an incident that had taken place. Although, in my heart, I knew that he was entirely decent and honest, I deliberately planted the seed of suspicion so that he would no longer be the center of attention.

He was deeply shocked and hurt. He could not understand why I would invent such malicious slander. I myself understood it only too well, and I tried to hide my own motives. As time passed, I realized how pathetic I was, and how nasty I had become. I also knew that there was an estrangement between us, a yawning gap I could not bridge because of my own pride. I simply could not bring myself to come to him and openly apologize.

Then, one day before Christmas, Stosh came to my house, and just as if nothing had happened between us, invited me to a New Year's Eve party at his house. "Jerry, it won't be as much fun if you are not there." I could not get over it! I, the sinner, should have forgotten my pride and come to him. Instead, Stosh came to me. Later, after becoming a Christian, I realized that this is just what God had done. When we sinful, prideful creatures could not bring ourselves to come to Him, He came to us through Jesus.

Jesus came down to the Jordan River to be baptized. He was spiritually driven to the river's edge not on behalf of His own sins, but on behalf of the sins of all humanity. He came to that place where John the Baptist was proclaiming the need for repentance. When John caught sight of Jesus, he cried out, "Behold, the Lamb of God, who takes away the sin of the world!" (John 1:29). As Jesus emerged from the water, he heard a voice say to Him, "This is my beloved Son with whom I am well pleased," (Matthew 3:17). In his heart, he knew. He knew that he was the long-prophesied Messiah (Savior, Anointed) whose task would be to bear our sins through His own personal suffering.

The prophet Isaiah had long ago inscribed these ominous words: "He was despised and rejected by men, a man of sorrows, and familiar with suffering. Like one from whom men hide their faces, He was despised, and we esteemed Him not. Surely He took up our infirmities and carried our sorrows, yet we considered Him stricken by God, smitten by Him, and afflicted. But He was pierced for our transgressions, He was crushed for our iniquities; the punishment that brought us peace was upon Him, and by His wounds we are healed. We all, like sheep, have gone astray, each of us has turned to his own way; and the Lord has laid on Him the iniquity of us all.

"He was oppressed and afflicted, yet He did not open His mouth; He was led like a lamb to the slaughter, and as a sheep before her shearers is silent, so He did not open His mouth," (Isaiah 53:3-7 NIV). Jesus presumably knew this prophecy and could anticipate his fate. Along with the joy of knowing the Father's favor comes the terrifying darkness. He was born to suffer the ultimate anguish: separation from God. This realization drives Him out into the wilderness.

Here He will be tempted. Many preachers and scholars visualize this simply as a scripture-quoting contest with Satan, the Adversary, the ultimate power of Evil. I don't see it that way. In order for temptation to be genuine temptation, it goes without saying that it must be tempting. There has to be something inherently appealing about it.

So, the temptation episode in the Gospel was not theater, not play-acting, but a seductive test of motivation. I think that the basic challenge coming to Jesus was a pathway out of suffering. That was the common denominator of the three appeals. Each alternative offered a "way out."

The first was to turn all of the stones into loaves of bread. The "grabber" was this: He could serve the Lord by becoming a social worker, and incidentally, He would not have to go to the cross. The second was to throw himself off the highest point of the Temple. In other words, if He specialized in miracles, crowds would follow Him, and incidentally, He would not have to go to the cross. The third was to become the Messiah everyone was looking for...the military champion. If He announced himself, ten thousand swords would instantly flash by His side, and He would not have to go to the cross. (Matthew 4:1-11).

We find ourselves asking the same question: Can I whole heartedly serve God and yet avoid personal suffering? It's almost like asking, "Can I swim without getting wet?" It's written in 1 Peter 4:12-13a NIV: "Dear friends, do not be surprised at the painful trial you are suffering, as though something strange were happening to you. But rejoice that you participate in the sufferings of Christ..." When all was said and done, and the battle fought and won, Jesus walked out of the wilderness with a pure heart and a clear head, spiritually prepared for a ministry which would end ignominiously in an excruciating death.

He preached the "Sermon on the Mount." It actually might have been comprised of the themes of many sermons all lumped together by Matthew (or his editors and redactors). So it could have been a literary device to assemble the core meaning of Jesus' preaching into one riveting "sermon." Our Lord was obliging each of us to examine our motives for our actions. There are three components to an action. First of all, there's the action itself. Secondly, there's the consequence. Thirdly, there's the motive behind the action. We tend to look at the action itself, and thus come off smelling like a rose, but God looks at our motive. As a pastor, I think my actions throughout my ministry have been mostly good, but my motives may have not been. Often, my motives stink. That's perhaps why the Psalmist could write, "O Lord, you have searched me and you know me." (Psalm 139:1 NIV).

In the beautiful Beatitudes, Jesus said, "Blessed are the peacemakers, for they will be called the children of God." (Matthew 5:9). We are forever misunderstanding these Beatitudes. This particular one says "peacemakers," and yet we persist in reading it "peacekeepers." It's usually easy enough for us to keep the peace. What requires greater risk is to *make* peace amidst anger, hostility, threats and perhaps violence. Yet, if you want to be a genuine follower of Christ, that's exactly what you have to do.

In the Sermon on the Mount, our Lord declared, "You are the light of the world...Let your light so shine that others may see your good deeds and praise your Father in heaven." (Matthew 5:14, 16). Christ Jesus himself is like the sun in our solar system, and we ourselves are like the moon. We cannot generate that solar energy, but we can reflect His light, His warmth, into the lives of others. Ours is but a reflected glory. We can't pick and choose to whom we will show love. We are absolutely commanded to love the loveless, the unloved, the unlovely, the unlovable. Jesus said that everyone loves people who love them back (Matthew 5:46-47). We are not everybody. We are to love even those who will *never* love us back. For this kind of unconditional love of which our Lord speaks goes beyond *feelings;* it is a resolute will.

Jesus' followers wanted some guidance on how to pray. He offered them what Protestants term "The Lord's Prayer," and what Roman Catholics term the "Our Father." We know the words from Matthew 6:9-13. The prayer is central to Christian worship. It has been regarded as "the model prayer." In other words, these are the petitions we should direct to the Lord. I disagree. I don't see it that way at all! If you stop to think about it, each petition represents a whole *attitude* that we are to inculcate into our lifestyle. For instance, we are to trust God enough to call Him "Father." Secondly, we are to be intent on glorifying Him in every aspect of our life so that His will may be accomplished in ourselves. Thirdly, we are to seek "our daily bread," that which is most necessary for us to live. We need to relinquish our own needs, seeking not what *we* think we need, but what He thinks we need. Since Jesus is "the Bread of

Life," our attitude should be that we seek Him most of all. That's what the journey to Jesus is all about.

Fourthly, we need always to be mindful of our sin, of our sins of omission and our sins of commission. Not only do we relish God's forgiveness, we extend that same forgiveness to others. Somewhere I read that whenever you forgive someone else, you set two people free. Jesus said that if you refuse to forgive that other person, God will not bother forgiving you (Matthew 6:14-15).

Fifthly, we trust the Lord to guide us either through or past temptation. Finally, we yield ourselves now and forever to this God who has revealed himself in Jesus. Therefore, the prayer is much more than a series of petitions. It's a compendium of the attitudes by which we must live.

In the course of His "Sermon on the Mount," our Lord said, "Do not store up for yourselves treasures on earth...but store up for yourselves treasures in heaven.... For where your treasure is, there will your heart be also." (Matthew 6:19-21 NIV). Once I quoted this to an adult Sunday School class I was teaching, when one young woman, Judy Donnelly, interrupted to say, "Notice He didn't say it the other way around." "What?" "He said. 'Where your treasure is, there will your heart be also.' Jesus didn't say, 'Where you heart is, there will your treasure be.'"

She was right. I had to think hard about that. Jesus had keen insight into human nature and knew that whereas our treasure doesn't always follow our heart, our heart will always follow our treasure. See, my heart is in children's hospitals, like St. Jude's, but is my treasure there?

Sadly, no. My treasure happens to be invested in various stocks. Is my heart there? You betcha! Our heart is guaranteed to follow our treasure; our treasure often fails to follow our heart. Given the fact that this is the way we humans are, Jesus is saying that we should put our treasure in the right places so that our heart will follow.

People occasionally say to me, "I'm not religious...I never go to church. I just try to live my life by the Sermon on the Mount." I used to congratulate them and say, "My, that's wonderful. I'm so proud of you." But now when I have grown into a cantankerous curmudgeon, I answer, "You live your whole life by the Sermon on the Mount? What does it say?" and they have no clue.

At the conclusion of His "Sermon on the Mount", Jesus told a story about two men. Each of them built a house. The first, a very foolish man, built his on sand. The second, with great wisdom, built his house upon a rock. Then a storm came, flattening the house built on sand. But the house built upon the rock stood firm.

I once heard a radio preacher comment on this passage. He said, "Perhaps both houses looked the same. They shared exactly the same architectural design. In fact, you couldn't tell the difference -- until the storm came." That's true with us too. When constructing our life, we focus on all the beautiful architectural ornamentation. Maybe, instead, we should pay more attention to its foundation. No one will be able to see any difference -- until the storm comes.

During His ministry, Jesus and His disciples were often on the lake we call the Sea of Galilee. It's the lowest freshwater lake in the world, teeming with fish. Remember, many of His followers were commercial fishermen, so they knew how to handle fish and how to handle a boat. Then in the middle of the night, a storm came up...a sudden squall, and they were terrified; Jesus was not with them. He had stayed behind on shore to pray. Try as they might, these professionals could not control their own craft. That has frequently happened to me in the course of my ministry. I encounter situations in which my customary reliance on my "street smarts" will not work, and I feel an inner panic.

Suddenly, their Master came through the storm, walking upon the sea, somehow transcending the storm. He spoke, "Take courage! It is I. Do not be afraid." He was saying, "I AM HERE." (Matthew 14:22-27). This episode will forever be indelibly engraved on my mind. I hope that old age and senility never erase it.

Helen Lemmel wrote:

"Turn your eyes upon Jesus,
Look full in His wonderful face,
And the things of earth
Will grow strangely dim
In the light of His glory and grace."[2]

Jesus said, "I am the light of the world. Whoever follows me will never walk in darkness, but will have the light of life." (John 8:12 NIV). It strikes me that when you turn on a light, you see three things. First, you see the light itself. Secondly, you see all the surrounding space, and thirdly, you can see yourself, all because the light switched on.

So it is when the Light of the world illuminates our life. That's how it was for me. At first, I saw Jesus' presence with me. With spiritual discernment, I was aware of a bright supernatural light. Then, I began to see everyone around me in a new light. I looked upon them non-judgmentally, with love and acceptance. Finally, I saw myself more clearly, as a child whom the Lord loves. Since then, my goal in this journey to Jesus has been not to fulfill my dream for myself, but to fulfill God's dream for me.

I once read a little story about a young boy who announced to his father that he would like to have a picture of Jesus in his room. Appreciating this very high-minded request, the father decided to fulfill his son's wish by taking him to a religious supply store. Now what the young boy specifically had in mind was one of those silhouettes of Jesus that was luminescent at night. Seeing that on his bedroom wall would bring the little boy great comfort.

However, he failed to communicate this to his clueless dad. The proprietor of the store showed the boy all of the pictures of Jesus that he had in stock. Each time, the boy emphatically rejected the proferred painting. Finally, exasperated, the store owner asked, "Well, just what kind of Jesus are you looking for?" to which he replied, "I want a Jesus who shines in the dark."[3] And that's the Jesus we get.

Jesus challenged those who walked with Him. He first asked them about the latest gossip. Who were people saying He was? His companions answered with enthusiasm, reporting the latest scuttlebutt. Then Jesus took them off-guard. "But who do *you* say I am?" There must have ensued an embarrassed silence. In a way, Simon Peter saved the day by blurting out, "You are the Messiah, the Son of the living God." (Matthew 16:13-16).

That is the question He's asking you and me. Our response is merely academic if we say, "You are the Messiah, the Christ, the Savior." That's like saying along with so many others, "I know there's a God," then adding parenthetically, "but there is no God for me. I know He's the Savior, but He's not mine." Nothing in our life will change until we can bring ourselves to say, "You are *my* Savior; I yield myself to *You*." Our Lord's question hangs suspended in mid-air like a chandelier, "Who do *you* think I am?"

One bitingly cold wintry weekend, I led a spiritual retreat for a large group of Presbyterian young people. The curriculum I was directed to use focused on Jesus being "Lord." As I was teaching, I was becoming painfully aware that the word "Lord" did not compute, that they did not really understand just what that meant. So I was simultaneously praying that something would happen to clarify that word. "Lord, please give me the key to unlock the mystery of who You are."

Then it suddenly came to me. I had the key! I stopped and asked them, "How many of you are on a sports team in high school?" I was amazed at the number of hands that were raised by both boys and girls. They were on track, cross-country, field hockey, football, baseball, softball, lacrosse, tennis, gymnastics, and more. "Who do you follow? Whose advice do you take? Who do you listen to?" and the answer came back: "The coach."

"The coach? You listen to your coach? Well, suppose your coach advises you to do something that you don't understand. What do you do?"

"We do it!" they chanted.

"Why?"

"Because the coach told us to do it!"

"But suppose your coach asks you to do something that doesn't make any sense to you? What do you do?"

"We do it anyway."

"Why? Even if it doesn't make any sense? Why do you do it?"

"Because the coach told us to do it!"

"And that is precisely what it means to call Jesus 'Lord'. Every decision, every action, is referred to Him. That's what it means to follow Him." We may not always understand His directives, but we follow them because we trust Him."

The earliest creed of the Christian Church is quoted in Philippians 2:5-11 NIV: "Your attitude should be the same as that of Christ Jesus: Who, being in the very nature of God, did not consider equality with God something to be grasped, but made himself nothing, taking the very nature of a servant, being made in human likeness. And being found in appearance as a man, He humbled himself and became obedient to death – even death on a cross! Therefore, God exalted Him to the highest place and gave Him the name that is above every name, that at the name of Jesus every knee should bow, in heaven and on earth and under the earth, and every tongue confess that Jesus Christ is Lord, to the glory of God the Father."

"Then Jesus said to His disciples, 'If anyone would come after me, he must deny himself and take up his cross and follow me. For whoever wants to save his life will lose it, but whoever loses his life for me will find it. What good will it be for a man if he gains the whole world, yet forfeits his soul? Or what can a man give in exchange for his soul?'" (Matthew 16:24-26 NIV).

My question is: what does it mean to "deny" oneself? I personally believe that Jesus was not focusing on our giving up "things" as much as He was focusing on our giving up our "self". He was telling us to *forget* about ourselves. Paradoxically, when I concentrate on denying myself, I become more conscious of myself than ever. So, it's counter-productive, self-defeating. Instead, if I focus on losing myself in others, I discover the liberating joy of life in a fuller dimension. The genuine cross-bearer (not the fake one who chooses an upholstered cross) is someone who is humble. I once read that true humility is not thinking little of yourself; it's not thinking of yourself at all.

We, who are so self-absorbed, need to think of others. Especially, we need to focus deliberately on that lonely and abandoned person who is typically ignored and by-passed. For Jesus once said, "Then shall the King say unto them on His right hand, 'Come, ye blessed of my Father, inherit the kingdom prepared for you from the foundation of the world: For I was [hungry] and ye gave me meat: I was thirsty, and ye gave me drink: I was a stranger, and ye took me in: naked, and ye clothed me: I was sick, and ye visited me; I was in prison, and ye came unto me...Inasmuch as ye have done it unto one of the least of these my brethren, ye have done it unto me." (Matthew 25:34-36, 40b KJV).

I hope that I never become so tone-deaf, so unconscious of others, that I fail to hear Jesus' "Inasmuch." I pray that I - and you - will never turn a deaf ear to the heart-rending cry of someone in need. In our journey to Jesus, we'd better not by-bass the wounded traveler on the side of the road!

One day Jesus told a parable we refer to as "The Parable of the Prodigal Son". In this story, the younger of two sons has sinned against his father and hurt him deeply. The son abandoned his father and journeyed far away from him. Finally, after realizing what he did, the son has made the decision to come back home. He has no idea how he'll be received but has carefully rehearsed a little speech he'll say upon arrival: "Father, I have sinned against heaven and against you and am no more worthy to be called your son." (Luke 15:18-19 NIV)

Jesus continued "But while he was still a long way off, his father saw him and was filled with compassion for him; he ran to his son, threw his arms around him and kissed him." And then the overjoyed father says, "For this son of mine was dead and is alive again; he was lost and is found." (Luke 15:24 NIV) Our Father in Heaven has been waiting for our own return. He comes to us even as we are coming to Him. He comes to us!

Now Jesus came to the end of his earthly life. He had come to Jerusalem to celebrate the Jewish Passover, along with his fellow Jews. They were remembering that awesome, awful moment in their Egyptian captivity, a thousand years earlier, when the Angel of Death struck down the first-born of the Egyptians, but passed over the dwellings of the Hebrew conscripted laborers. They had obeyed God's instructions to slay a perfect unblemished lamb and paint its blood over their doorways. This no-account tribe of nobodies did just that, and were saved by the blood of the lamb. (Exodus 12:1-13)

The chronology between the synoptic Gospels (Matthew, Mark, Luke) and John's Gospel differs. According to John, Jesus appears to have celebrated a day earlier. It is possible that Jesus ate the Seder meal one evening before the rest of the population ate theirs (there have probably been many scholarly attempts to reconcile this.) Why would Jesus have celebrated with Seder a day earlier? Perhaps because He knew that by the next evening He'd be dead. Because the lambs were not yet sacrificed, I'm guessing that Jesus' entourage did not eat lamb on the night that came to be called "The Last Supper." That means that Jesus himself was the lamb.

Remember how, at the beginning, John the Baptist had proclaimed, as he first saw Jesus approaching, "Behold the Lamb of God who takes away the sin of the world!" (John 1:29).

During the meal, our Lord offered the bread: "This, my body, for you." Then He offered them the cup: "This, my blood." In this act, which we do in remembrance of him, is the heart of the Eucharist, the Mass, the Lord's Supper, Holy Communion. Different faith traditions call it by a variety of names. Essentially, Christ is offering himself to us.

I had a good friend, Charlie Evans, who once served as a Roman Catholic priest and eventually became a Methodist pastor. I talked with him one day about his experiences and understanding of this crucial ritual. "Charlie, when you were a priest did you believe in the Eucharist?"

"Of course," he said.

"And when you became a Methodist minister, did you believe in our act of Holy Communion?"

"Certainly. I believe in them both. What I affirm is the Real Presence of Christ in the offering of bread and wine."

He continued, "When I attended St. Charles Borromeo Seminary, they explained to us that Transubstantiation is, at heart, a mystery. I could appreciate that. A mystery is something that cannot be explained. Then they made the mistake of trying to explain it. Don't tell me *how* Jesus is present in the Eucharist; tell me instead how it should affect my life." We are so interested in living our own life. He is interested in our living His.

On the night of the Last Supper, Jesus spoke of Eternal Life: "Do not let your hearts be troubled. Trust in God; trust also in me. In my Father's house are many rooms. If it were not so, I would have told you. I am going there to prepare a place for you. And if I go and prepare a place for you, I will come back and take you to be with me, that you also may be where I am." (John 14:1-3 NIV). St. Paul, quoting the prophet Isaiah, later wrote: "'No eye has seen, no ear has heard, no mind has conceived what God has prepared for those who love Him.'" (1 Cor. 2:9 NIV, quoting Isaiah 64:4).

It's true that we, with our finite brains, cannot conceive of anything other than this world in which we live. We live within four dimensions (if you count 'time' as the fourth), but we cannot picture a world of five dimensions or more. The Bible employs metaphorical language to help us to understand. Humility dictates that we admit that our own understanding of God's promises is bound to be limited. We just trust God.

I once read the story of a young pastor who was sent to a church that had a living saint nicknamed "Brother Jenkins." This old man had memorized vast portions of scripture, whereas the young pastor did not have the same command of his material. One day the pastor received word that Brother Jenkins was dying. He hurried to his house and sat by his bedside. This old man said, "Son, I know that I'm dying. All my life I've banqueted on God's promises, and just now I can't remember any of them." The young pastor spoke, "Just now, neither can I, but what is important is not that *you* remember the Lord's promises or that *I* remember the Lord's promises. All that really counts is that the *Lord* remembers His promises!"[4]

There's an Epiphany hymn I've always loved, "As With Gladness Men of Old." The last verse really speaks to my heart:

"Holy Jesus, every day
Keep us in the narrow way;
And when earthly things are past,
Bring our ransomed souls at last
Where they need no star to guide,
Where no clouds Thy glory hide."[5]

When the Seder had concluded, Jesus and His followers journeyed out from the Upper Room and made their way to the Garden of Gethsemane, where Jesus would struggle mightily in prayer. Once more the primal temptation came to Him and ensnared His soul. The possibility of escaping His destiny! Maybe He still could escape this sacrificial death on a cross. He was in such extreme anguish that the Gospel writer Luke noted that "His sweat was like drops of blood falling to the ground." (Luke 22:44 NIV). The shadow of the cross was so close that Jesus could reach out and touch it.

Then the trap set by the members of the religious orthodoxy was finally sprung, and Jesus was captured.

Throughout the long night, He was shoved from one authority to another, accused of blasphemy. It was a capital offense, but the religious establishment was not permitted to administer the death penalty; only the Empire of Rome could do that. Jesus was accused of claiming to be God. The Roman Catholic New Testament scholar, Brant Pitre, remarked that no one was crucified for claiming to be the Messiah. But one could be executed for the blasphemy of claiming to be, in some way, God.[6] So Jesus was dragged before the Roman Prefect, Pontius Pilate, charged with a political crime: treason. He had implied that He was "King of the Jews." See, the accusation had been cleverly shifted from "blasphemy" (which Pilate would not have cared about) to "treason" (which he would). For the crime of treason, Jesus would be sentenced to die. Strung up between heaven and earth, suspended in empty space, He was dying the death of a common criminal.

When preachers preach about the cross, they invariably focus on the excruciating physical pain of crucifixion...the nails driven through flesh and bone, the raw wood rubbing on a whip-lashed bleeding back, the thorns pressed into the brow, the whole body pulled and stretched. None of that can be denied. Yet the greater pain was spiritual. Here was the Son, who was so much a part of His Father, now separated from him for what must have seemed like eternity. Jesus was separated, alienated, isolated not by His own sin, but by ours.

There's a prophetic passage written in Isaiah 59:1-2 NIV perhaps hundreds of years before Jesus' birth: "Surely the arm of the Lord is not too short to save, nor His ear too dull to hear. But your iniquities have separated you from your God; your sins have hidden His face from you, so that He will not hear." In Isaiah 53:5-6 NIV, it says, "But He was pierced for our transgressions, He was crushed for our iniquities; the punishment that brought us peace was upon him, and by His wounds we are healed."

Jesus spoke these mysterious words: "...I lay down my life...no one takes it from me, but I lay it down of my own accord." (John 10:17-18 NIV). Most people understand these words metaphorically, but in my sanctified imagination, I see them literally fulfilled. One did not simply hang limply on the cross. That's the way we always picture it, and apparently it's incorrect. In order for the crucified victim to breathe, He had to lift himself up on the cross, despite the punishing pain that it would produce. Then, in His resulting weakness, He'd slump down once again. These movements continued until it became a rhythmic motion on the cross. When our Lord said, "It is finished" (John 19:30a NIV), I picture him simply lowering himself on the cross and refusing to continue pushing himself up to exhale.

"With that, He bowed His head and gave up His spirit." (John 19:30b NIV). In other words, true to His assertion, no one took His life from him; He literally ***laid it down*** Himself. "Father, into your hands I commit my spirit." (Luke 23:46 NIV). Long ago it had been written, "For a brief moment, I abandoned you, but with deep compassion I will bring you back. In a surge of anger, I hid my face from you for a moment, but with everlasting kindness I will have compassion on you..." (Isaiah 54:7-8a NIV).

Isaac Watts looked at the figure on this cross and in 1707, wrote:

"Were the whole realm of nature mine,
That were an offering far too small;
Love so amazing, so divine,
Demands my soul, my life, my all."[7]

Jesus overcame His death. He was alive again in a strange, new way. We speak of "spiritual bodies" and "glorified bodies." We can't comprehend it. How did it all transpire? How did it shake down? I myself have no idea, having nothing to compare it to, but I know that somehow He is alive, not in our precise sense of being "alive," yet He is *real*. He transcends the dimensions of our world, and He has made God real to me. I cannot put him under a microscope or a telescope (I am under *His*), but my own life has been transformed. "For God, who said, 'Let light shine out of darkness,' made His light shine in our hearts to give us the light of the knowledge of the glory of God in the face of Christ." (2 Corinthians 4:6 NIV).

Finally, our response to Jesus requires faith. There are a zillion definitions of that little word "faith." Yet, I have always appreciated this acronym: F-A-I-T-H, meaning "Forsaking All, I Trust Him." That's it. Through life and death, if we live, the Lord is with us. If we die, we'll be with him. Once you say "Yes" to him, you are inseparable. Once He said, "...and whoever comes to me I will never drive away." (John 6:37b NIV)

On the first day of the week, Mary Magdalene crept in the pre-dawn darkness to the tomb (John 20:1). To her dismay, she saw that the stone had been rolled away. She just stood there, completely empty. Becoming aware of a presence behind her, and supposing him to be the gardener, she heard him ask, "Woman, why are you crying?" She answered, "Sir, if you have moved the body, please tell me where..." He spoke one word, "Mary!" He called her by her name, and she knew the Risen Christ (John 20:11-16).

When I was a teenager seven decades ago, I would have liked to meet Jesus, an inspirational teacher. He was one of my heroes. I did not, as yet, believe in any kind of resurrection. You might say that I revered a dead hero. But so did Mary Magdalene, if you think about it. She was journeying to Jesus to pay her respects to a dead hero. She did not find Him; He found her. Serendipitously, she met not a dead hero, but a living Savior.

The journey to Jesus is an adventure. You might traverse mountains and valleys, mountaintops and wildernesses. Nevertheless, through the highs and lows of life, it's an adventure. Always remember that as you are journeying to Jesus, He is journeying to you! He comes to you and to me. He comes to us.

Albert Schweitzer famously wrote: "He comes to us as One Unknown, without a name, as of old, by the lakeside. He came to those who knew him not. He speaks to us the same words, 'Follow thou me,' and sets us to the tasks which He has to fulfill in our time. He commands. And to those who obey him, whether they be wise or simple, He will reveal himself in the toils, the conflicts, the sufferings which they shall pass through in His fellowship, and, as an ineffable mystery, they shall learn in their own experience who He is..."[8]

## FOOTNOTES

1. Hymn "I Know Not How;" text by Harry Webb Farrington (1880-1931); words © 1921 by Harry Webb Farrington.

2. Hymn chorus "Turn Your Eyes Upon Jesus;" words and music by Helen H. Lemmel; 1922.

3. "Knight's Treasury of Illustrations;" Walter B. Knight; "A Christ who shines in Darkness" (Grand Rapids, MI: Wm. B. Eerdmans Publishing Company, 1963); p. 203.

4. Basic story (which I adapted) found in "Three Thousand Illustrations for Christian Service;" Walter B. Knight; William R. Eerdmans Publishing Co.; Grand Rapids, Michigan; © 1947 by Wm. B. Eerdmans Publishing Company; Eighth printing, November 1967; "When We Forget," p. 228.

5. Hymn "As with Gladness Men of Old;" text by William C. Dix; (1837-1898); verse 4.

6. "The Case For Jesus: The Biblical and Historical Evidence for Christ;" by Brant Pitre (professor of sacred scripture at Notre Dame Seminary in New Orleans), published by Image, an imprint for the Crown Publishing Grp, a division of Penquin Random House L.L.C., New York; © 2016 by Brant Pitre; pp. 10, 142, 157-158, 163.

7. Hymn "When I Survey the Wondrous Cross;" text by Isaac Watts; verse 4; 1707 (Gal. 6:14).

8. "The Quest of the Historical Jesus;" Albert Schweitzer; MacMillan; New York; 1910; p. 401; First German Edition: "Von Reimarus zu Wrede;" 1906; First English Edition published in Great Britain by A. & C. Black, Ltd.; 1910.

Scriptures noted "NIV" are taken from the "Holy Bible," New International Version, NIV. Copyright © 1973, 1978, 1984, 2011 by Biblica, Inc. Used by permission of Zondervan. All rights reserved worldwide, www.zondervan.com.

Scriptures taken from "The Message" Copyright © 1993, 1994, 1995, 1996, 2000, 2001, 2002. Used by permission of Nav Press Publishing Group.

## Other titles from Higher Ground Books & Media:

Love's Resurrection by Daniel K. Held

Redeeming Gethsemane by Daniel K. Held

Raven Transcending Fear by Terri Kozlowski

Oasis or Mirage by Terra Kern

The Deception of 666 by Terra Kern

Breaking the Cycle by Willie Deeanjlo White

Man Made by Grace by Willie Deeanjlo White

Healing in God's Power by Yvonne Green

Chronicles of a Spiritual Journey by Stephen Shepherd

Eyes of Understanding by Stephen Shepherd

Wise Up to Rise Up by Rebecca Benston

Bits and Pieces by Rebecca Whited

Finding Purpose in the Pain by Brenda W. McIntyre

The Real Prison Diaries by Judy Frisby

The Words of My Father by Mark Nemetz

Add these titles to your collection today!

http://www.highergroundbooksandmedia.com

## HIGHER GROUND BOOKS & MEDIA IS AN INDEPENDENT PUBLISHER

### Do you have a story to tell?

Higher Ground Books & Media is an independent Christian-based publisher specializing in stories of triumph! Our purpose is to empower, inspire, and educate through the sharing of personal experiences. We are always looking for great, new stories to add to our collection. If you're looking for a publisher, get in touch with us today!

Please be sure to visit our website for our submission guidelines.

http://www.highergroundbooksandmedia.com/submission-guidelines

## HGBM SERVICES IS OUR CONSULTING FIRM

### AUTHOR SERVICES

HGBM Services offers a variety of writing and coaching services for aspiring authors! We can help with editing, manuscript critiques, self-publishing, and much more! Get in touch today to see how we can help you make your dream of becoming an author a reality!

*****

We also offer social media marketing services for authors, small businesses, and non-profit organizations. Let us help you get the word out about your book, your projects, and your mission. We offer great rates, quality promos, consistent communication, and a personal touch!

http://www.highergroundbooksandmedia.com/editing-writing-services

## Need Bulk Copies?

If you would like to order bulk copies of this book or any other title at Higher Ground Books & Media, please contact us at highergroundbooksandmedia@gmail.com.

We offer discounts for purchases of 20 or more copies. Excellent for small groups, book clubs, classrooms, etc.

Get in touch today and get a set of great stories for your students or group members.

www.ingramcontent.com/pod-product-compliance
Lightning Source LLC
Chambersburg PA
CBHW061518040426
42450CB00008B/1677